BLOOD WASHING BLOOD

BLOOD WASHING BLOOD
A Zen Perspective of
Psychotherapy

RAY MENEZES

JANUS PUBLISHING COMPANY LTD
London, England

First Published in Great Britain 2005
By Janus Publishing Company Ltd,
93–95 Gloucester Place
London W1U 6JQ

www.januspublishing.co.uk

Re Printed 2008

British Library Cataloguing-in-Publication Data
A catalogue record for this book
is available from the British Library

ISBN: 978-1-85756-584-3

Cover Design: Janus Publishing

Printed and bound in the UK by PublishPoint
from KnowledgePoint Limited, Reading

Thank you to Karen Wrack and Liz Claridge for their help in editing the manuscript early on.

For Cathy, Dionne, Sean and James with love.

"Clearing thoughts from the mind as they arise is like washing away blood with blood. You may succeed in washing away the original blood, but you're still polluted by the blood you washed in."

"If you just let thoughts come and let them go away, and don't put them to work or try to avoid them, then one day you'll find that they've vanished completely into the unborn mind."

Bankei

"The real world is beyond the mind's ken; we see it through the net of our desires, divided into pleasure and pain, right and wrong, inner and outer. To see the universe as it is, you must step beyond the net. It is not hard to do so for the net is full of holes." (contradictions)

Sri Nisargadatta Maharaj

Contents

Introduction

This book is the product of my own journey, it is not meant to be an autobiography, although most of what follows has come from personal experience. My journey has been long and hard. I have been forced, sometimes kicking and screaming, to find the source and meaning of my pain. It has sometimes felt like a conspiracy; if I get it wrong it hurts, if I get it seriously wrong it seriously hurts. In solving my own pain I stumbled upon certain principles that seem to me to explain what is going on. Why do we experience pain? What exactly is pain? What is real and what is unreal? Who am I? Why is the world in such a mess and why are so many people in so much pain?

What follows is distilled from my life, all my life experiences of pain or joy. It has come from the people I have been fortunate enough to meet. By this I mean all the people I have met; there is no such thing as a human being I cannot learn from.

Although the information I am presenting in this book is essentially very simple, it seems that the mind finds it very difficult to hold. I believe this is because the mind has a rather fixed view of reality and of the rules that govern our sense of who we are and what the world is. More simply perhaps, the part of us that tries to understand the ego is the ego and the ego can only comprehend that which is of the ego.

Of necessity what is written may seem sometimes repetitive. This is intentional. I am attempting to communicate to the ego and to that which lies behind the ego. I believe that the ego wants to help but that it needs to be convinced of the truth of what is being said. To this end, both in this book and in my work as a psychotherapist I attempt to communicate using a language that is sometimes repetitive. My intention is not to be repetitive, but to find new ways of saying the same thing. To this end also, I have included a number of Zen parables that again use language to point to something that is beyond language and meaning.

1

Beginnings

So there I was, drowning within sight of paradise. My life did not flash before my eyes. In the space of a few moments I found I had moved from a state of extreme fear to one of profound stillness. It was as though the world had stopped. In my fear I could see nothing, now I could see everything. There are fish swimming all around me as I sink. Their form, their movement and most of all their colours entrance me. I am completely still and have no desire to move or resist.

The water is crystal clear and the sun's rays are reaching down through the water and caressing the ocean floor. Coral reefs rise before me in the distance. Within the stillness I become aware of the possibility of reaching this coral and now I have the strength and the will to reach it. Now I am standing on the coral and breathing again, my mouth is only just out of the water. I am looking towards the beach; it is early morning and there seems to be no one around.

Something has happened to me. I remain completely still within, there is no fear. I wait, feeling the waves gently lapping around me. There are no thoughts; there is only the observation of the world around me. When my breathing returns to normal I slowly and gently swim back to the beach. I remember who I was before this incident but now I am someone else. Before I had been in great emotional pain and had wanted to die. In those few moments in the sea this all changed. It was not that I now wanted to live; now the question does not arise.

One year later I am walking up a mountain path in Dharamsala, India. Up ahead I see a Tibetan monk walking down the path towards me. It is almost as though he has come to meet me; he walks down the path directly towards me. He only stops when we are face to face. He is smiling at me as though I were his long-lost son; he clasps my hands in his and shakes them. Then he walks on down the mountain never looking back.

I never saw him before and I have never seen him since, yet this man has had the most profound effect upon me. Again, everything occurs in a matter of minutes and all that appears to have happened is that a man stops and shakes my hands.

I felt as though for the first time in my life someone had accepted me totally and unconditionally. I had not thought such a thing was possible. This man saw something in me that I had been unable to see for myself.

One week later I am walking in the mountains and as I come around a bend in the rocks I find myself face to face with what I believe to be a snow leopard. We are about twenty feet apart; the leopard stands there and looks at me. I look back and strangely I feel no fear. This continues for what feels like a few minutes then the leopard slowly turns around and walks away; after a while he begins to run. I am astounded by the ease and strength of this animal as it jumps over huge boulders until it is lost from view.

The Big Bang

For many years I had a recurring lucid dream in which I found myself in a large two-storey house. I felt wide awake and knew I was dreaming. Beginning on the upper floor, I explored the house; there were many rooms. I took time to look in each room. I appeared to be looking for something. Having looked in every room on the upper floor I went downstairs and continued my exploration. The last door on the ground floor led to a cellar. I went down into this cellar and found a room that was carpeted; it did not look like a cellar. There was another door in this room that I walked over to. I opened the door and there was absolute darkness. The darkness is so complete it almost appeared to be another door. Without any hesitation I closed the door.

I understood this dream to mean that there was something in myself that I could not face. Even though I am exploring the house and clearly looking for something, when I come to this room in the cellar my searching stops. I was not aware of feeling fearful or anxious in the dream. It was almost as though the fear was so great that there was no question that I would close the door. It is also significant that I do not feel afraid and yet clearly my response of closing the door suggests that I am very afraid.

On some level I feel that I always knew what this dream was about. There were other clues in waking life that link to the dream. I remember walking along a road with a friend, it is a beautiful sunny day and I remark to my friend how good it feels to be alive. At the very moment that I complete this sentence a bird swoops down in front of a car that is passing and falls close by my feet, dead.

Even as I write this now it is almost as though I am recounting a dream, but this was not a dream and there were many other recurring events of this nature.

Many years later, during my psychotherapy training, I discovered the meaning of the recurring dream and life events, but not in any way I would have expected. I had been in therapy about three years. My therapist and I were both interested in Reichian body-work. I also was interested in body-work through my practice of Vipassana meditation, which has two parts. The first part focuses on scanning the body and noticing the physical sensations that arise in the various parts of the body. The second part involves focusing on the breath as one inhales and exhales.

There came a point in my therapy where my therapist and I agreed that it was the right time to do this. The body-work involved regular deep breathing and focusing my attention on a sensation I was feeling in my chest. I held my hands over this area of my chest and my therapist placed his hands over my hands and applied pressure. He then encouraged me to allow a sound to arise from this area.

Very quickly I entered an altered state. My face and lips felt numb and after a while I began to experience intense sensations running through my body almost like electric shocks. My body began to shake and suddenly I was crying, but not like I had ever cried before. It felt like a tap had opened in my eyes and tears flowed copiously. I was not aware of any thoughts at this time. There seemed to be no obvious reason for my tears. The tears and physical sensations continued for most of the hour session.

In my next session, we continued this work with exactly the same result. By the end of this session I had reached a point where the tears began to stop of their own accord, not because I wanted them to stop. At various times after these sessions memories began to arise like bubbles of air that had been trapped beneath the sea, that had somehow been released and now floated to the surface. Some of these memories were not new but there was something different about them. They were more detailed than I ever remembered before; more importantly I seemed to be feeling these memories as though the events were happening now.

One memory that rose to the surface allowed me to see and feel what was behind the blackness that I had closed the door on in my dream; I found I was re-experiencing a particular time in my childhood. I was experiencing this time as though I was actually there. The time was not long after my family had moved from east London to north London.

I was about nine years old and had recently started at a new school where I was very happy. In this memory I found myself walking home from school. It was a beautiful sunny day and I remember feeling an intense feeling of joy just to be alive. As I approached my front door it suddenly opened and my mother appeared; she was screaming and her face was covered in blood. I felt paralysed; everything seemed to be happening in slow motion.

I was aware that somewhere behind my mother was my father (I could not see him); I was also aware that he had done this to my mother. I felt a huge sense of anger; I wanted to kill him and at the same time felt utterly powerless to do anything. I believe now that this feeling of rage towards my father could not be acknowledged and that rather than blame him it was easier to blame myself. Something inside of me died in those few moments.

My mother grabbed hold of me and demanded that I take her to a hospital, which was about three miles away. We had to walk as we had no money. I remembered people staring at us all the way to the hospital, but no one offered to help. At the hospital we found that my mother was not badly hurt, the blood had all come from a cut above one eye. Apparently, my father had thrown a teapot at her.

Now I understood the door in my dream and the beautiful sunny day, where out of the blue a bird dropped dead at my feet.

Blood Washing Blood

If there is one central idea behind this book it is in these three words, blood washing blood. What follows hinges on the meaning of these words.

As a young man I believed that anything could be solved, if only I could organise the information correctly, like the completed picture of a jigsaw puzzle that would all become clear when the last piece is added. There are many problems with this view, especially when the puzzle in question is my life. What are these pieces that need to be fitted together? Are they memories? Are these memories accurate? If the memories are not accurate then what will the finished picture look like and will it have any meaning? If I use other people's information, how much can I trust that?

The incidents in my life mentioned earlier do seem to me to be parts of a puzzle. The near death experience in particular has challenged me for many years. So much changed in my life after that experience. In some sense it did not matter to me what the meaning of the experience was; I was and am grateful that it happened. Yet there is a part of me that feels it is important to understand what actually took place in that short time in the sea. The solution was not mystical or spiritual in nature; it was very simple and straightforward. I stopped resisting. I began to relax and accept who I am and what the world is – not in an intellectual way, but as a fact. I began to observe myself and the world without adding anything to the observation.

So what was the part of me that was resisting and why? The part that resists is the ego and I believe that in understanding the nature of the ego we come to a solution as to why we need to resist.

Since Freud, there has been much written about the ego; what is said can be quite daunting and complex. I prefer to look for a simpler way of understanding the nature of the ego. It could be said that the ego is the part of me that resists. What does it resist in particular? Pain, in all its forms, is the simple answer to this question. To understand the ego it is necessary to understand pain. What actually takes place when we experience pain and what does it mean? If I burn my hand I will experience a physical sensation that initially seems to demand that I remove my hand from whatever it is that has caused this sensation.

So the first part of the meaning of pain is that something is wrong. What went wrong occurred at a specific moment in time. I do not experience the sensation prior to this moment in time, so clearly what went wrong can be narrowed down to a specific moment. This information leads me to the correct conclusion that something I did caused something to go wrong. The sensation therefore tells me I have done something wrong and also what I have done wrong and when I did it. After understanding what went wrong and why it went wrong and having corrected it (removed my hand from the offending object), I find that the sensation continues. So what is the purpose of this? Something is obviously still wrong.

What is still wrong is that although I have removed my hand, the burn remains untreated. The sensation of pain continues until some action is taken to acknowledge and repair the damage, even then it may continue for some time, as the healing process itself can be painful. Even when the pain is most intense it is possible to feel the pain and at the same time not resist it. Pain is directly related to the degree to which we resist; the more we resist the more intense the pain.

All of this also applies to emotional pain. The pain tells us something is wrong, it even tells us when it went wrong, if we are awake enough to notice. Emotional pain is much harder to locate than physical pain. With a burn there is no doubt as to when and where the pain occurred and what the pain feels like. With emotional pain we may not know when or where the pain occurred and the pain itself may be more in the nature of a general sense of foreboding. Nevertheless all the information we need is there, we only need to look more attentively and become more sensitive to the ways in which the body communicates this type of pain.

If we know when the pain began then we may have clues as to what may have caused it. It is not always obvious as to what it is that causes emotional pain. It is also not so important to know the cause; processing the pain does not require that we understand the pain.

It is the nature of the ego to resist pain. It is not the pain that is the problem so much as the ego's solution to the pain. The ego's solution to the pain is to resist.

The resistance can take the form of denial: 'I don't have a problem'. It can take the form of replacing the problem with another problem as with alcohol, drugs, crime, or violence. All of these are ways to avoid a simple fact: we hurt.

It is not pain that is the problem – it is the ego; it creates an even bigger problem by trying to solve the hurt that is experienced. This is 'blood washing blood'; the problem itself tries to solve the problem.

The ego's solutions have a tendency to create bigger problems. Money, power, fame, sex, violence, many forms of mental illness and even religion are used by the ego to solve the original problem, which is simply that we hurt.

To solve our problems, emotional or physical, it is necessary to understand the nature of the ego and its methods of avoiding pain. These methods almost always involve power; that is, how power is lost and the ego's methods of regaining it, whatever the cost. What follows is an attempt to clarify all the ways in which the ego seeks to make itself indispensable, while at the same time creating chaos in our lives. This is followed by an exploration of the ways in which we may by pass the ego to access a part of our self that is more able to solve the apparent or actual problems we are faced with in life.

The First Punch

As a child growing up in the East End of London, my mother instilled in me the notion that if any other child was to pick a fight with me I should always get the first punch in. I guess she was trying to protect me. Unfortunately it did not work out that way.

Very soon after starting school I began to experience bullying. On my first day at one particular school, I remember my brother and I going out at playtime and being confronted by a number of other children (it seemed like all the children in the school). I have no recollection of why, but these children began to attack my brother and me. My brother and I fought back to back until a teacher intervened. I am pretty certain now that the only reason this happened was due to my darker skin colour.

A pattern began to appear. I changed schools many times and each time I turned up at a new school the bullying would begin. I began to get the first punch in. As soon as I became aware that I was heading for a fight I lashed out as hard as I could and punched the other boy in the face. But here is the strange part – after having punched the other boy in the face I would give up, usually I would lie down on the floor and get beaten.

It took me many years to figure out what was happening. As a teenager I got into a fight with another boy and was about to go through the same sequence, when I suddenly realised what I was doing; for some reason I was predicting the outcome and my prediction was that I would always lose.

This time I did not lose and later I began to understand what had been happening. My mother had told me to get the first punch in but said nothing about the second punch. I had taken the information literally and got the first punch in but then stopped. I am put in mind of programming a computer; the computer cannot perform a function it has not previously been programmed to do; it does exactly what it has been told to do.

13

The learning for me in all this is that children have a tendency to take the information they receive from their parents (and others) literally. The information that my mother had given me was not just that I should get the first punch in. Implicit in the information was the idea that I would always have to fight to survive. It was only with my experience of drowning that I was finally able to put this myth to rest.

I was watching a programme on television recently in which a father was talking about his son who had murdered a number of elderly people. At one point the father was telling a therapist that he had been very strict with his son but that he had always loved him. The therapist responded by saying that although she believed him when he said he loved his son, she did not believe that this was what the son had experienced. The father, with tears in his eyes, acknowledged that although he did love his son, love was probably not what his son had experienced.

We do not feel loved because someone thinks they love us or because they tell us they love us. Love is not related to what we are given. Love is not conditional. If we are loved because we are clever, bright or because we are well behaved, it is conditional; often there is the implication in conditions that if we are not clever, bright, or well behaved, for instance, we will not be loved.

Love is acceptance on a very deep and consistent level. It is not conditional and therefore it is not easy. The child always knows if they are loved or not. I remember someone saying that the child experiences love when they see their parents' eyes light up on seeing them. The child needs to feel accepted regardless of whether or not they are clever, beautiful or well behaved. They need to feel accepted for no other reason than that they exist. All of this applies equally to adults, and in all relationships. We cannot thrive without this kind of love, which is exactly why there is so much suffering in the world. Without this kind of love we cannot begin to accept ourselves, let alone anyone else. We cannot move on until this problem is addressed. It can only be addressed when we begin to take responsibility for the fact that we may not have been loved in the way we wanted to be loved. If it did not happen there is not much point to wishing it had; we cannot change history, although most of us spend our lives trying to.

Blueprints

Why would we not want to learn? Surely we would not want to choose something that would cause us pain? Yet we clearly do make choices that consistently cause us pain. The reason for this is, I believe, because of the way that the child absorbs information. From the beginning the child is subject to an ever-increasing torrent of information. By information I mean all contact that occurs between the child and the world, all the impressions that are received by the body, all words, sounds, images, smells, touch, taste and all sensations.

How does the child begin to process or organise this information? The answer to this question is 'badly'. How does the child distinguish between what is true and what is false? How does the child understand something that cannot be understood? The answers to the last two questions are 'it cannot'. The child has no means to distinguish what is true and what is false and often accepts something that is false as true. Maybe the best example of this is when the child accepts, because of certain information received from its parents, that it is unlovable. Parents may love their child yet still the child feels unlovable. For the child, his belief about whether he is loved or not is determined by his perception of reality. Not necessarily the truth, but rather what the child perceives to be the truth.

When parents divorce, for instance, although both parents may continue to love the child as before, for the child something has dramatically changed: one parent is no longer with him.

The child is not interested in logic or reasons, only facts. The most important fact for the child is that now, one parent is no longer with him, or with him less than before. The child has its own logic, completely unrelated to adult logic. In this instance, the child's logic says, 'My father is no longer with me. If he loved me he would be with me; if he is not with me it must be because he does not love me.' And further, 'If he does not love me then I must be unlovable.' Obviously, this must also be true in regard to a mother not being with her child.

15

Or it may be that the parent does not love their child; then the child may seem justified in feeling it is unlovable. The fact that a parent does not love their child does not mean that the child is unlovable, it means that the parent is not capable of loving.

Nevertheless, the child now believes this false information and may continue to do so for the rest of its life. This information has now become a blueprint. It is imbedded in the brain cells and has become truth, albeit a truth that is untrue.

All future actions and beliefs arise from this blueprint. They arise even though consciously we try to choose something different. The conscious mind has no power over the unconscious mind. The unconscious mind tends to choose the exact opposite of what the conscious mind chooses. An example of this would be when the conscious mind chooses to forgive while the unconscious mind continues to hate.

Blueprints state precisely what the rules are; if the blueprint states that you are unlovable it does not mean 'sometimes', it does not mean that if you find someone who does love you that you will suddenly feel lovable.

The blueprint is almost absolute; it is not subject to change unless the feelings that caused the blueprint in the first place are fully processed or experienced.

A blueprint is taken by the child to be truth. Perhaps this is because the child has no prior information about reality; the child has no reference point by which to compare information.

A major part of our blueprint is taken from our parents. If we are male, our mother represents the feminine; she becomes our model of what the feminine is and how we will relate to that model. That model will, in the future, be projected on to all women and we will act out certain scenarios that relate not to these women, but to our mother. Consciously, we may avoid choosing someone who is similar to our mother, while at the same time unconsciously choosing someone who is either very much like mother or someone who can (unconsciously) be manipulated into becoming her.

Father, on the other hand, represents the model of the masculine and, if we are male, he represents us as well as all other males in our life. Again, we may consciously resist being like our father. Sometimes even choosing to do things that are opposite to the way he would do things.

There is no escape however; sooner or later we find that we are very much like him.

A child, like a computer, can only operate according to the information it is given. In the beginning it is not a question of choice, rather it is a question of what information we have from which to make choices.

For women, mother is the model of themselves and all other women in their life, although some women will match mother more closely than others. Father will represent all aspects of the masculine; how she relates to him will determine how she relates to all men. If father was not there, the information about the masculine is limited. This does not mean it is missing – even no information in this case is information. This information will usually consist of an assumption that men are not to be trusted, that eventually they will leave and that she will always get hurt by them. Again, there is a very strong tendency to either choose men who will embody these distorted aspects of the masculine or choose someone who can be (unconsciously) manipulated into fitting our concept of what the masculine is. This is all very strange; we may wonder, 'Why do I always choose men who hurt me?' It is difficult to see that we choose exactly what we want and what we expect and that all of this has already been determined in the way that our blueprint of the masculine was formed.

Why do so many men hate, abuse, rape, or even kill women? And why do so many women hate men and feel the need to punish them in various ways? The answer is contained somewhere within the blueprint.

Blueprints are not open to discussion; they are almost absolute. The more we deny them the truer they become. This is because our denial is untrue and being untrue, a state of conflict is created. Conflict ensures that the thing denied is reinforced.

To be free of a blueprint it is necessary to acknowledge the information it contains, completely. When we do this we begin to see the truth and because we no longer deny the truth, we free ourselves from conflict. This, in turn, allows our blueprint to naturally fall away. As it falls away, we begin to discover who we are and what the feminine and the masculine really are. Who we are is the truth behind the smokescreen that is our blueprint.

What Are You Rebelling Against?
What Have You Got?

It is very natural that at some point the child begins to rebel. The child must at some point, cross over from the child identity to the adult identity. How does the child get from one side to the other? We all have to make this journey, but not all succeed. Age does not automatically confer adult status, although many believe that it does.

The child rebels in order to become an adult, but also wants the advantages and perks of being a child. This is observable in the world – people appearing to be adult but behaving like children, sometimes very young children. They may have children of their own, hold responsible jobs, appear to be adult in every way, but when looked at closely it becomes clear that it is all pretence and that behind the pretence is an adolescent still rebelling against mother or father or both.

Obviously, this begins to look slightly ridiculous if we are still literally rebelling against our parents when we are forty-five years old. However, rebelling against our partner or boss, or against our government, or against other nations, politics, religious beliefs, in fact anyone else, can satisfy this need. We can always find a valid reason to rebel, reject or hate. The fact that we have transferred our rebellion on to any of the above seems to go unnoticed unless our rebellion escalates to a point where we break the law.

As all of this has been going on for thousands of years and is fairly universal today, it almost appears normal. Groups are composed of individuals, so it is not difficult for groups or nations to act out this rebellion in the form of war, terrorism, or crime.

I believe that it is our life's purpose to complete the process of moving from the child identity to the true adult identity. It could be said that this is the goal of most religious and spiritual paths. Not completing this process becomes increasingly dangerous for the world and for us.

Where to begin? First of all, this is all about responsibility – taking absolute responsibility for one's self. This is not easy; in fact, it goes against everything we believe. We are required to see that the problems we have are ours and not to do with anyone else. You might say, 'Well, it can't just be me– other people can do bad things.' This is true, but we are not responsible for what they do, only what we do in response or, more importantly, what we feel in response.

If you feel angry when someone rejects or insults you, the 'normal response' is to reject or insult back. This is because of the feelings, or more specifically the physical sensations that arise when we feel rejected. We don't want these feelings and unconsciously we convert feelings into thinking; this takes the edge off our feelings and gives us a sense that we are doing something to take back control.

When we react to these feelings we create an alternate universe in which everything appears back to front. We have temporarily lost touch with reality.

Not surprisingly, this tends to be confusing and we may make mistakes and escalate the problem. This can occur if I insult or reject someone because I feel they have rejected me. If we could take responsibility for our own feelings we would not have to go through the escalating phase. The feelings belong to and are created by us.

It is a question of attitude; if I feel angry I will not assume that someone else has caused it. I will assume that (for some reason I may no longer be aware of) the feeling has originated within me. Often, angry feelings are related to low self-esteem, so in a sense when someone insults or rejects me I am not angry because they reject me, but because I already believe that I am not acceptable. The other person is merely reminding me of this fact. I do not wish to be reminded! So I distract myself by attacking back, or making the other person feel what I am feeling.

For most children, communicating what they are feeling is almost impossible; it is difficult enough for adults. So what to do? Again, the unconscious steps in and comes up with a very clever solution. What is it that the child might wish to communicate that would be so difficult?

A child usually has no problems communicating that they are hungry, tired, happy, or even, to some degree, sad. If the sadness is uncomplicated, as for instance, when the child is refused a treat, there is then no long-term problem. If however, the child feels unloved, then something very complicated has occurred that will require a more complex, subtle and long-term solution.

Initially the child is faced with the problem of communicating his intense feelings of rejection. The child is usually unable to express these feelings verbally but has no problem expressing feelings non-verbally. Non-verbal communication requires action; it requires that the child's behaviour is modified in such a way that the person who is being communicated with, will feel what the child is feeling.

If the child feels unloved, then it is very likely that the child will behave in ways that cause mother or father to feel what it is like to feel unloved. This is very easy for the child; he can become disobedient, lie, steal, swear, play truant and generally be difficult.

At this point, if the parent is able to understand the communication (rather than reacting to the problem by punishing the child), then it is still possible to rectify the problem. If, however, the parent does not understand the communication and punishes the child, the problem begins to escalate out of control; the child has no alternative but to up the stakes. This could involve bed-wetting, nail biting, anti-social behaviour and ultimately, what would come to be seen as a mental health problem such as depression, obsession, neurosis, or even psychosis.

All of these behaviours may be the result of the child finding ever more extreme methods to communicate what he is feeling. It is likely that when the child becomes an adult, these early behaviours will undergo a transformation; they will become more sophisticated, more 'adult'. The behaviours may now take the form of alcohol or substance abuse, criminal tendencies, or long-term mental health problems.

The Language of the Ego

The ego is a defence system designed to protect us from pain. In essence it is a very simple system. It protects us from pain by helping us forget anything that it considers painful. This is taken a step further by avoiding anything that might remind us of this pain. The ego comes into existence as a result of pain or, put another way, as a result of a loss of power. It is therefore natural for the ego to see things in terms of losing power or gaining power.

I believe this defence system does not in fact protect us at all. The ego sees defence as being in control; not being in control implies a loss of power. For the ego it is of no consequence whether it really is in control or not, it only needs to appear to be in control. For the ego, the best form of defence is attack or control. When we are in great danger we may pray to God to help us even though we might not actually believe that God exists. This is my point: it does not matter whether or not God exists, it only matters that we have something to hold on to. In this case what is held on to is an idea. This is a very powerful idea; it allows us to reinvent reality to suit our supposed needs. For this system to work, a mechanism is required that can conveniently help the right hand to forget what the left hand is doing. This mechanism is the ability to forget what the left hand is doing. It is as though the ego has invented a form of amnesia that can be used at will and whenever required to serve its purposes.

Included in this mechanism is the ability to create time. Time distracts us from what is real. Time, in this context, is duration and measurement. All language is about time. Words are put together in a sequence that implies time.

This is much like music; a note alone is not music, it is sound. It becomes music when it is placed in a sequence with other notes. We need to be able to remember notes that no longer exist. In music there is only one note or notes played at the same time that can exist in any moment. The music we hear is always a memory of what no longer exists. The mind is fooled into believing that what it hears is music, rather than one continuous sound. Memory, used in this way, enables us to hear and appreciate the music. Even when looking at a painting, photograph, or sculpture, memory is needed to organise the details of colour, form and context.

This principle is important for the ego; it needs to be able to create a world that can be wonderful and seductive, a world that we can believe in and be distracted by. After listening to Mozart (or whatever music touches us), how could we doubt the seductiveness of this illusion?

Power involves the creation of strategies and defences designed to avoid or diminish pain, while at the same time restoring the illusion of power. This power is untrue because it is created as a means to feel powerful, rather than to truthfully be powerful. It is also untrue because it is arrived at through a misapprehension of an event in our life that caused us pain. For example, when a child's parents get divorced.

This is a catastrophe for the child, whatever the reasons; the child has lost a parent. A child's perception of this kind of event is often that he is responsible for the parent leaving. The child believes that it is he that has been left rather than his mother or father. The child feels and is powerless; he does not have the means to understand what has taken place. It is hard enough even for the parents to understand what has taken place, much less the child. Faced with the intense pain that this event produces, the child is forced to protect himself.

This protection is given over to the unconscious mind because the unconscious mind can arrive at solutions that are unthinkable to the conscious mind. The unconscious mind has the ability to create strategies ranging from relatively mild anti-social behaviour such as truanting, swearing, or disobedience, to the child harming themselves or others. If necessary, the child has the option of resorting to 'madness' as a penultimate means to regain power. The ultimate act of power is to commit suicide.

Some years ago, while working in a psychiatric unit, I witnessed one of the most powerful acts I have ever seen. I was in an observation room, observing a family therapy session. A young boy I will call David had been a patient in the unit for some months; he was considered to be psychotic. In the family meeting was David, his mother and father, a family therapist, a social worker and a nurse. David seemed to be relatively 'normal' during the early part of this session. He sat quietly and appeared to be listening attentively.

As the session progressed, David's father began to get angry, raising his voice when talking to David's mother soon he was shouting at her. Suddenly, he stood up and began kicking her.

I was watching David very closely at this point; as soon as his father started kicking his mother, David began to exhibit the crazy behaviour that had caused him to be admitted to the unit. He began shouting, his words made no sense; he was waving his arms and kicking his legs wildly. I saw that David was sacrificing himself for his mother. As he began to behave crazily, all the attention in the room moved to him; his father forgot about attacking his wife and began to attack David. This all happened very quickly and nurses soon had the situation under control.

I began to wonder if David really was psychotic, or unconsciously using a strategy designed to protect his mother. Over the years I saw many examples of how inventive children and adolescents can be in their strategies of regaining lost power.

The proof of our imperfection is experienced every time we are reminded of how our power was lost. It is re-experienced in our bodies as physical sensations. The arising of these sensations forces us to employ again the strategies for regaining power that were created in response to our original loss of power. These strategies involve the avoidance of unwanted sensations through the activity of thought, which in turn creates solutions involving the regaining of power by false means.

It is necessary to accept and fully experience these physical sensations without acting upon them, thereby not continuing on this loop.

A huge amount of energy is expended in keeping this system operational. If we can find a way of ending this cycle, the energy is freed up and made available for the body, resulting in increased levels of perception and feeling and decreased levels of anxiety and fear.

This is definitely possible, although our mind or ego will do everything in its power to prevent it. It is like cornering a wild animal; the animal may not want to attack but may be driven to it by its need to protect itself. It is important to approach the animal with compassion and with no intention to cause it harm.

Principles of Power

Power is experienced as a sense of wholeness. If as a child we experience anything that diminishes that sense of wholeness, it will be experienced as a loss of power.

Diminishment of wholeness may be caused by rejection, physical, sexual, or verbal abuse, the death of a family member, or any event that causes the child to experience mental or physical pain. It is inevitable that we lose power because it is inevitable that we experience pain.

It is the degree to which we lose power that determines whether we are a saint or a sinner, a depressive or a neurotic, a schizophrenic or a psychotic, an alcoholic or a drug addict.

The degree to which power is lost determines the degree to which we will need to regain it. To this end, there is no strategy too extreme that will not become valid if necessary.

Extreme methods of regaining power are not always predictable as we are all uniquely different and will experience similar events in a wide variety of ways. That is to say we will regain our power in ways that are unique to ourselves.

Due to the function of the ego and the nature of thought, we see ourselves and others as good or bad, right or wrong, powerful or weak, ugly or beautiful. These are incorrect assumptions and in no way apply to the nature of reality.

Real power exists prior to thought. It manifests most clearly in our senses, in our sight, hearing, touch, taste and smell. It manifests especially in the way these senses work together to guide us through life.

We are most powerful when we are very young. Paradoxically, this is the time when we are most vulnerable. When vulnerability encounters pain, as it must, we are propelled into the world of power.

The first element of power is to repress all unacceptable feelings, thoughts, memories and physical sensations. Thought itself is our primary line of defence. When it is active, the physical sensations (which are the reason we need a defence in the first place) are subtly diminished.

The secondary modes of defence are the strategies employed by thought such as smoking, eating, drug-taking, angry and violent behaviour, to name but a few. To focus on secondary defences as though they are the problem is futile.

When an infant experiences hunger, cold or discomfort of any kind he finds that screaming or crying are ways to restore order. As any parent knows, this strategy is truly powerful. A child now has a weapon to combat any pain or anxiety that may arise. A child also begins to realise that this weapon or power can be used for other purposes.

A child uses simple but irrefutable logic: life involves pain; pleasure is the absence of pain; therefore, if I can attain pleasure, I can avoid pain. This becomes our life purpose and all our energies are devoted to this goal.

As adults we continue to use the logic of a child; however, we are no longer children and the logic no longer applies. The medium of this logic is thought and we believe that any solution to our problem must come through this medium. Thought is itself the problem and thought has decreed that only by using thought can we resolve our problems.

The inherent problem with thought is the ultimate catch 22. In Zen Buddhism this problem is sometimes referred to as 'Blood washing blood'. All attempts to improve or change one's self come under this heading; it is as futile as trying to wash a blood-stained garment in blood and expecting to clean it.

If I try to improve myself, I am already in conflict with myself – it is like a dog wishing to be a cat. Trying to change myself without first resolving this inherent conflict cannot work. Even if I appear to have changed, the underlying conflict makes sure that it will not last; more changes will have to be made. Complete understanding of this principle is vital, for if it is not completely understood we must inevitably continue to try to solve our problems with the problem itself.

The origin of conflict is in our unwanted feelings. If these feelings are not processed, we must inevitably fail in our effort to change. Processing these feelings means accepting them completely, physically and mentally.

Unwanted feelings are the truth we attempt to deny through the pursuit of change. In this there is a movement from the present to the future in which who we are is rejected in favour of who we would like to be.

The person we would like to be can never exist, because this person always resides in the future. We prefer to reside in the future because the present or the truth of who we are is intolerable. That which is intolerable must be faced if we are to be free of pain and fear.

The intolerable has two aspects: mental and physical. Of these, it is the mental aspect that poses the greatest difficulty. The mental aspect has the capacity to create total pain and fear.

Pain and fear are caused by our ability to reinterpret reality. That is, an ability to conceive of and to experience something that does not actually exist. A simple example of this is anything we have decided we like or do not like.

Not liking something can set in motion all kinds of problems. If we decide we do not like emotional pain, we can decide to like smoking, drinking, eating excessively, or drugs, even though these new choices can create even more emotional pain. I use the word choice because we are responsible for what we do regardless of whether or not we remember what we have chosen. That is, we have to live our choices. *There is a Zen story about a samurai warrior who goes to a Zen master asking to be taught about heaven and hell. The master tells the samurai that he is too stupid and that he would not waste his time teaching him anything. The samurai is enraged and begins to draw his sword; the master says, 'This is hell'. On hearing this, the samurai puts his sword back in its sheath; the master says, 'This is heaven'.*

It is clear from this story how our own thoughts can lead us, within moments, to either heaven or hell. Sanity or insanity is based on the degree to which we believe our own thoughts. If our thoughts are consistently negative we move towards depression. If thought decrees that life is too difficult, it becomes a fact and we become depressed.

We view ourselves and the world through the lens of thought; if our thoughts are positive then our view of life is likewise positive, if our thoughts are negative then so is our view of life. I am not suggesting that we replace negative thinking with positive thinking; thought is thought, regardless of whether it is positive or negative. In this sense, positive or negative thoughts are exactly the same.

Thought itself is tolerable; it is the physical sensation behind thought that we cannot tolerate. It is this physical sensation that causes us to think. It is assumed that if we have a problem we need to think our way out of it. This assumption usually indicates that thought is the only option available. If a problem is a mathematical or scientific problem, it is valid. If on the other hand, it is an emotional problem such as, anger, sadness, depression, or death, the solution of 'thinking our way out of it' is unlikely to work.

There are times in life when, if we were dependent on thought to solve our problems, we would probably be dead. Drowning was, for me, one example of this. Another example would be when driving a car and being faced with a situation that does not allow me the luxury of time to think out a solution and implement it. Also touching something very hot demands that I remove my hand immediately.

Thought is usually too slow to be effective in these situations and the problem needs to be handed over to a part of myself that can act instantly and correctly. I think of this part as the body, but it can also be thought of as the right hemisphere of the brain. This part of the brain is not usually called on to solve these problems because the left hemisphere has priority, being the dominant part of the brain.

In the West in particular, most of our schools, colleges and universities value this part of the brain more highly than the right side. I think of the left side of the brain as the part that deals with bits of information – one and one make two, for instance. It is the part that thinks and that draws on memory. It is the part of our brain that is concerned with the past. The right hemisphere of the brain I see as being concerned with using all the information that is entering our mind and body through the senses right now. The amount of information being received is phenomenal. This is a very different order of computing than 'one and one make two'.

The left side of the brain can be seen as very clever, but essentially uncreative. The right side can sometimes appear stupid – as with idiot savants – yet is essentially intuitive and very creative. Ideally we need both these hemispheres working in harmony. There is reason to believe that meditation can correct the imbalance between the left and right hemispheres of the brain.

The reason that the physical sensation we experience is so difficult to deal with is that physical sensation or pain is not an isolated entity. If it were, we would only have to deal with a limited amount of discomfort or pain.

What if all the emotional pain of our lives is stored in the body as physical sensation and when we experience some kind of emotional pain in the present this is somehow connected to all the emotional pain of our lives? The ego would consider this too much pain and would immediately begin implementing various strategies to avoid this backlog of emotional pain.

My definition of ego is simply a mechanism designed to protect us from physical or emotional pain. This protection is never real; in fact, this so-called protection can take the form of mental illness, substance abuse and even death, as in the case of suicide. The ego genuinely believes it is helping; it does not understand that it is itself the problem.

The strategies of the ego are all related to thought. There are two main categories: primary thought and secondary thought. Primary thought is thought itself regardless of content. That is to say, it is thought itself, any kind of thought, positive or negative that is the primary defence mechanism of the ego.

Secondary thought is the particular content or strategy of thought that is designed to reinforce the primary aspect of thought. Simply put, when we are faced with emotional pain our first instinct is to think, to try to find some solution through thought. To some degree the solution is immediately found in that thought itself has the effect of diminishing physical feeling. The act of thinking is the act of control. The solution we are looking for is to avoid or diminish pain and so the act of thinking is already a partial solution to pain. The secondary aspect would be, for instance, the thought 'I need a cigarette'. You can replace 'cigarette' with any number of other devices designed to diminish emotional pain.

Trying to solve secondary thought means we have already bought into the ego. We are trying to solve a problem on the ego's terms. Blood washing blood!

If we can focus on primary thought – thought itself – we will not be distracted from the real problem and therefore be that much closer to a solution.

Krishnamurti often told his audiences this story. The devil and a friend are walking along a road when suddenly the devil stoops down and picks something up. The friend asks, 'What was that you just picked up?' The devil replies, 'It is truth.' The friend asks, 'What do you intend to do with it?' The devil replies, 'I will give it to mankind.' The friend says, 'Surely that will be bad for business?' 'Oh no,' says the devil, 'I will help them organise it.'

It is not truth that is the problem, rather it is the manner in which we organise it. The way in which we organise truth almost always involves dualism. Dualism is the act of adding something that is not inherently there; for instance, when we describe a sunset as beautiful or rainfall as depressing. They are neither; they are ways of organising information, but not necessarily truthful ways.

Is it always necessary to organise information in this way? When there is a valid purpose, such as information related to science or technology, then yes. But what is the purpose of describing a sunset as beautiful or rain as depressing? It is as though we are convinced that unless we actually say or think this thought we will not have actually experienced the sunset. It is in some way a loss of faith, a product of insecurity.

Is it possible to experience anything without describing or naming it? It is not that there is not beauty in a sunset, rather that when we endow something with beauty we necessarily take it away from something else. What is it we see when we view something that does not live up to our high ideal of beauty? Often it is the opposite of beauty – ugliness or disharmony.

Primary thought has the function of distracting us from anything physically or psychologically painful. This includes even mild discomfort. Another function of primary thought is to create the illusion that we are in control.

Pain is seen as bad and as having no positive result from experiencing it, even though, within science and medicine, it is known that without pain we would be in great danger, as is sometimes the case with medical conditions where the pain receptors are switched off. Still, in general, we consider pain negative and usually do all in our power to suppress it. The reason for this is, I believe, two-fold.

First, pain is unpleasant; it appears quite reasonable to not want to feel it. If pain was pleasant it would not serve the same function; to help us distinguish that something is wrong, maybe even life threatening.

Second, all pain is related to all other pain, both physical and mental.

If we experience any pain, the potential exists to experience all pain. When I say all pain, I am referring to all the unwanted or repressed pain of our lives. Many of us now understand that any pain that is repressed can become physically locked into the body. This can then manifest as various symptoms of the body.

If all pain is connected to all other pain, it becomes possible to access pain from the past that we may not even be aware of. Pain from the past can be accessed and processed through pain from the present. Pain can only be processed if there is no attempt to deny or repress it. In fact, not attempting to deny or repress pain is the process.

The moment when the pain of the past is accessed, is the moment when we experience the pain of the present and make no attempt to deny it. This moment is not experienced in any way that the mind or ego can recognise. It is invisible. There is nothing to measure with, because at this point we are not trying to deny or assert anything. There is, then, no frame of reference.

It is an act of faith to access and process pain in this way. Because it involves feeling rather than 'thinking', it is a journey without distance. At some point, this act of faith is rewarded with a new sense of freedom that has a life of its own, a life that is not dependent on thinking or knowledge.

Power lost must be regained at any cost. In some ways power can be seen like entries in a ledger: there are credits and debits, the books need to be balanced. If a child experiences some form of abuse or rejection, power is debited, resulting in the immediate need to re-balance the books.

A child has no instructions or guidelines on how to process his feelings of vulnerability, he therefore makes up his own instructions; he fiddles the books. He cannot get back the power that was lost, so he settles for taking back someone else's power or doing something that invests him with a feeling of power that will temporarily satisfy him and at the same time appear to balance the books. The books are, however, not balanced; they only appear to be. The strategy to take someone else's power or to do something that invests us with a feeling of power must be constantly repeated in order to maintain the illusion.

When losing power we are propelled into a dream-world where our sole purpose is to regain the power that was lost. There is a feeling of absolute need to redress the balance, so much so, that there are often few inhibitions as to what we will or will not do to this end.

The only way we can actually lose power is to give it away or believe that it has been taken. If someone insults you, for instance, it can only hurt if we believe the insult to be true. If we believe an insult to be true, we experience a feeling that tells us we have lost power. It does not matter at this point that it is our own belief about ourself that causes us to experience this loss of power. The belief is an illusion, but the feelings that arise are experienced as real.

Physical or mental action must be taken to regain equilibrium. It is most likely that this action will reflect the event that caused the loss of power or equilibrium in the first place.

The feeling that correlates to the perceived loss of power is one of total loss or grief, like the death of a loved one. Except in this instance, the loved one is oneself.

We need to feel powerful or, put another way, we need to feel in control, even if this control results in something harmful to ourselves.

The need for power and control is clearly evident in the world. Individuals, families, groups, or nations time and again repeat the same errors resulting from the need for power, or from the reaction that arises due to the loss of it.

Errors occur when power is taken away; our usual response is to take it back. Again, the means of taking power back tends to be in a similar manner to the way in which it was lost.

If someone insults us, we are often compelled to insult the person back or to find some other means to take power; possibly internally or simply thinking badly about someone is an effective means of taking power back. The other person does not need to know, we know.

If someone takes power from us and we then take it back, the person is compelled to find another means to again take power. This time, however, they have a good reason – you have taken their power away. It does not matter who started this power game; it always begins somewhere down the line with someone perceiving that power has been taken away.

In extreme situations the stakes get higher and higher, resulting in violence or even war; the stakes are increased until there is no recourse but to kill.

We still cannot win. We now have to live with the fact of taking someone's life and also the fact that someone else (individual, family, group, or the state) may wish to avenge the death. In the case of nations this violent game may continue for thousands of years. The nation that wins the war loses the war. The nation that loses the war is compelled to find a means to get back or get even. It is not over.

What is the damage to the psyche of nations that embark on war? It is similar to the damage done to the psyche of individuals who kill, only far more complex and subtle. Not only can we not win but also, we inflict great damage on the psyche of the nation and of the world.

What happens to soldiers returning from war? Do they switch off from the psychopathic state that may have been necessary to win or lose the war, or even to survive the war? What is the result for the world of all the wars that have ever been fought?

For surviving losers it is necessary to find another way to win or take back power, if not in an overt way, then in a subversive way. Resentment, hatred and anger are all related to power and can be passed down through generations.

To resolve the problem of power retrieval, we need to experience fully the feelings that losing power entails and to let go of the wish to take power back. Although thinking and feeling can affect each other, it is necessary to isolate one from the other and to be able to move freely between them. Vulnerability is required if we are to fully experience the feelings that losing power produces.

Vulnerability is feeling exactly what we feel in any particular moment without the addition of thought or meaning. When we are truly vulnerable we become truly powerful; we enter a state of truth. At this point, there is no further need for defence and as defence is the major function of the ego, the ego becomes redundant.

Feelings and Sensations: the Gateway to Truth

It seems to me that the body has been much maligned over the centuries. It is punished in the name of God for being what it is: sexual, mortal and animal. Even the Buddha and many Zen masters succumbed to this view before their awakening.

When we have a problem we automatically hand it over to the ego, the probable cause of the problem in the first place. No matter how disastrous the ego's solution might be we always go back to it for more punishment. In fact, the ego's solution to most problems is to punish the body. Think of all the creative ways the ego does this; alcohol, cigarettes, drugs, all kinds of self-harm, anorexia, bulimia, violence to self or others, all forms of mental illness and the deprivations that can arise from them, dieting, over-eating – there is no end to this list.

Far from being the unclean unhelpful part of us, the body is in fact the part of us that lives in direct contact with truth. This is the truth that is experienced by the body in the living moment, prior to the interpretations given to it in the following moments.

The body is supremely intelligent, it knows when it is hot or cold (and exactly how hot or cold); it knows when we need to eat, sleep and expel bodily waste. It knows how to regulate the heart, something the mind is incapable of doing. It knows how to navigate itself through the world, up and down stairs or mountains, in and out of doors and mostly without error.

This all may sound very simple but what is involved in these simple functions of the body is nothing short of miraculous. Most of these miraculous capabilities of the body are taken for granted. We look to higher abstract knowledge as being more important. It is important, but not more important. It is worthless if we are not alive to appreciate the higher abstract knowledge.

The body is always in direct contact with truth; the world and the body naturally reside in truth just as they are, prior to the addition of thought.

All the pain of our lives is stored within the body. It is stored in the body and needs to be processed by the body. The ego's response to this pain is to suppress it. This may help in the short term, but finally we have to pay the piper.

This payment can be in the form of mental or physical illness, dysfunctional relationships and generally contributing to the insanity of the world. It is like having a toothache and putting off going to the dentist. Eventually we lose the tooth and in the meantime we suffer.

Begin to look on your body as your friend. Trust that it holds all the information that you will ever need. Begin to know your body, not from an intellectual point of view but directly, physically. Know it as you would know that something is hot. If something is very hot we don't stop to think about whether or not we should remove our hand or not. We simply remove it.

The part of you that removes your hand is the body, not the ego. As I said, begin to know this part. At first this is very difficult, we habitually want to use our intellect to understand how we feel.

Again we need to trust that there is another part to us that we have access to. It is much easier to notice when something is very hot. We have no choice. We are forced to notice. Noticing how you physically feel right now in terms of physical sensations is not so easy. It is as though we need a big sign to tell us that we have a body.

Take some time right now to notice what you are physically feeling. Begin with any obvious sensations, any aches or pains. Then go deeper, is the body hot or cold, try not to think about it, actually experience it. Notice the more subtle sensations that are always occurring throughout the body, the tingles and twitches.

Notice any stresses or strains in the way you are sitting or standing. If there are pains or aches begin to explore them, notice how the body tenses up when it is in pain, how the muscles almost physically try to push the pain away. Explore the boundaries of the ache or pain. Begin to explore the possibility of relaxing into the pain, accepting the pain totally as it is. Do this on the physical level. Notice the tension and relax it. Try not to name the pain; don't see it as pain but rather as sensation. Don't measure the degree or intensity of the sensation.

Every sensation of the body is to be considered important, regardless of its origin. Generally, the more subtle sensations of the body are harder to discern but easier to allow once contacted, while the more extreme sensations, such as pain, are easier to discern but harder to allow.

The body holds a vast amount of information about our relationship to the world and others. This information is usually denied us simply because we don't know of its existence. We only become aware of it when we experience pain and even then we tend to reject it. Any pain or sensation can become the gateway through which we can process the pain of the past.

It Don't Mean a Thing
(If it Ain't Got That Swing)

Imagine yourself split in two. Let us call one part the physical and the other part the ego; the part that gives meaning to what we experience and the part that tries to protect us from any negative feelings. The physical you is the part that can be seen and touched, it is the real you. Imagine the ego part of you sitting in a chair beside you; this part is invisible, it cannot be seen or touched by you or anyone else. The only way this ego part of you can appear to exist is when it can convince or trick itself or others that it does. This trick is very simple; it is the ego's ability to believe its own imaginings or thoughts. Once this is achieved, it has no problem convincing others that it exists, as most others are busy using the same trick.

The ego part of you is invisible, but is the part of you that gives meaning to the world. It is the part that determines if a thing or experience is good or bad, ugly or beautiful, right or wrong. Now be aware of the physical you, the part that can see, hear, touch, smell and taste, this part is separate from the part that creates meaning. It is entirely physical.

When we inhabit the physical body without the part that creates meaning, there is only what is, or truth. Truth is never good or bad when experienced by the body alone.

There really are these two separate parts and it is possible to move between these parts at will, according to which part is relevant or appropriate in any given moment. We do not need to continually give meaning to the world, as though if we did not the world would cease to exist. If you touch something hot you do not need to think it is hot to enable you to move your hand. The body knows very well what is hot and will take the appropriate action.

There were a number of clues to this in my early life, where I found myself in situations in which there was not time to think; the body needed to act instantaneously to survive. When I was drowning, it was not thinking that saved me but the absence of thought. My body saw the world clearly and truthfully and was able to act upon that perception. That perception did not involve fear.

Fear arises from the part that creates meaning. The body does not experience the world in terms of meaning; it experiences the world in terms of physical sensation.

The world comes into being at the point where the body and the world meet, that is, in the senses. Some believe that without the part of ourselves that constructs meaning we are merely a piece of meat. This is not true; the body is intelligent in its own right – it is only because it is dominated by the ego that we rarely get a chance to see what it is capable of. There are times where it is absolutely appropriate to impose meaning on the world, but the meaning itself is never absolute, it is a work in progress.

We need to apply meaning to the world very sparingly and even when we do, we need not be dominated by it. More important still is the ability to reside in a world without meaning. This does not mean a meaningless world or a nihilistic world but a world prior to meaning, where the world is its own meaning.

It seems to me that there are two aspects to a human being. There is the body/mind, which includes the body and the brain, and there is the ego.

I do not see the body/mind as two separate parts. They function as one, most noticeably in the way breathing and the heart are regulated. The mind and the body usually function perfectly so that we do not have to concern ourselves with breathing; we simply breathe. This is a simple statement for a very complex operation. It is interesting to note that when I recommend the awareness of breathing as a meditation practice, people find that this is very difficult because the ego tries to take control. The ego cannot sit back and observe the breathing process, it wants to be involved.

Likewise, the heart manages to beat, usually the precise amount necessary to keep us alive; in some cases this is for more than a hundred years. The other aspect to being a human being is the ego. Ideally the ego is a tool; it supplies us with information that can help us survive. This includes everything from language to technology. When this tool is used well it can achieve the near miraculous. Look around at what it has achieved; from making fire to travelling to the moon.

There are all the wonders of science and of art, music and architecture. But let us look also at the negative side of this. We can build frighteningly powerful weapons that we are quite prepared to use. We have fought wars for thousands of years; we have found endlessly 'creative' ways of killing and torturing each other. Every day there are more horrors and many of these we can now watch on television. Sometimes I feel a deep sense of shame that I am a part of the human race, not because I believe I am any better but because I recognise that I am a part of it. I believe this darker side of being human is entirely to do with the ego and its need to take power from others as a way to elevate itself.

Principles Involved in Working with Feelings and Sensations

When a feeling or physical sensation is completely experienced, the intellect or ego is naturally excluded. Feelings need to be experienced directly and fully through the sensations that arise in the body prior to thought. It is our incomplete feelings that allow the ego to become involved; this results in the ego producing 'solutions' to problems it has no ability to solve.

All the emotions such as anger, grief, happiness, etc. are correlated by physical sensations. By the time we label these feelings 'anger', 'grief', or 'happiness' the physical sensation is old. The label comes after the sensation; it is the ego's attempt to protect itself or us from this sensation, as well as to prove that it is in control and therefore that it exists. These feelings or sensations are real and need to be experienced.

Thought arises from the ego in order to protect us from body sensations that are considered to be painful, uncomfortable, or unnecessary.

The intellect or ego is usually the dominant part of the mind. That is it has priority over the body in solving problems. For most people, it is not only that the intellect is dominant but that we are unaware of any other option. The body is the other option but this is dismissed by the ego as it is prone to feeling too much. We cannot feel too much, we can only think too much.

Feelings in themselves are without meaning; the meaning comes after the feeling and is produced by the ego. Meaning gives the ego a way to take control of unwanted feelings. There is no limit to the amount of meaning or interpretations of reality available to the ego.

If we could separate meaning from feeling and focus on feeling, we would begin to realign ourselves with the world as it is. We can experience this sometimes when working physically, when what we are doing takes on a life of its own. Physical work usually requires less thought. If we can fully engage physically with what we are doing, thinking diminishes and there is therefore less conflict. In Soto Zen there is an emphasis on physical work, I believe, for this reason.

The times when I have most felt this have been when I have been in physical danger and have needed to act.

Think of meaning the way an artist thinks about colour. We might, for instance, think that green is the colour of grass. While this is true, it is only one possible meaning. Green may also be the colour of the sea or the sky, in fact it may be the colour of almost anything; its meaning is not in its colour but in the way that the artist chooses to use it.

Meaning is not absolute, it is relative. Meaning is determined by its context and it is always temporary. I choose to give something meaning for now but may not always choose to do so. Thinking needs to be more flexible; if it is too rigid we become slightly crazy, we begin to believe our own thoughts.

Death

When thought arises we enter a dream in which fear, pain and death exist; none of these exist prior to thought. Prior to thought, fear and pain exist as body sensations only. Prior to thought death has not occurred, it can only be a dream of the future. This is not to deny the death of the body, only the psychological impact of the concept of death on our lives.

Death is something we can have ideas about, but cannot know. It is always in the future, for if it arises, we are already dead and no longer able to say what it is or is not.

It is not death we are afraid of, it is life. Death is literally unknowable, so if we are afraid of death, our fear must arise from within life. Fear of death arises when the ego dreams of the future. The ego is afraid not that we will die, but that it will die.

There is death in every moment as phenomena arise and pass away. Nothing is permanent, all things and all life are in the process of arising and passing away. The universe, with all its galaxies, stars, planets, moons and life, will all pass away. Not only in the future but now.

Thought is a solution to the unacceptable fact of death; with thought there is continuity with one image or thought, connecting to the next image or thought. It is this mechanism that we use to deny the immensity of death. We need to keep the continuity between thoughts running, for if there is a gap we will be faced with this 'unacceptable fact'.

It is the mind's ability to record, store, playback and link thought or data together that creates the illusion of time, space and movement. When the mind creates time, space and movement it is experienced as utterly real. We can touch, taste, hear, see and think about it. The illusion is complete except for one detail; pain, in all its forms, mental and physical.

Whether mental or physical, pain tells us that something is wrong. Not only that something is wrong in terms of an external problem, but something is wrong with our interpretation of reality. We only get to this perception when there is enough pain; there is not usually enough pain because the ego is so good at suppressing pain.

Only something extreme like death or the collapse of certain illusions can get past these defences of the ego and arrive at the next stage of knowledge.

Being born, we enter a world that is, in truth, unknowable; we then spend the rest of our lives denying this fact. The unknowable nature of the world is most clearly represented in death. There is no data available when faced with death, so the mind resorts to using data from the past, in an attempt to resolve the conflict and the pain that is experienced. Nature abhors a vacuum.

In a near death experience it can happen that the data from the past also does not work and so the mind or the ego collapses; there is no data available to resolve this problem. Using this data from the past is an act of desperation.

The truth is there is no data that can help us resolve our feelings of pain and conflict. The fact that we are trying to solve anything is the problem in the first place. If we are trying to solve something then we have already created a state of conflict. A conflict between that which is and that which should be. As long as we believe that it is possible to resolve our inner conflicts using information from the past there is no hope of change.

The illusion of knowing is overwhelming. Wherever we look we literally see the concrete fact of this knowledge. We are surrounded by proof that this knowledge is real and works.

When faced with death we are faced with the contradiction that the knowledge we trust so much cannot solve this particular problem.

To say I believe something is true is to say I do not know if it is true. If in fact, I do not know, why does it become necessary to continue with a belief?

We need to believe because there is something to be gained from doing so. We get to create a world that is more to our liking than the world as it is.

We have a tendency to believe what we want to believe, what gives us comfort, what we find acceptable and what we hope for. Most of all, we believe because it is too uncomfortable to accept that we do not know.

Is it really so terrible not to know? Does it mean chaos and disorder? Does it mean death? If what we know is false, then not knowing becomes ultimate wisdom.

Our civilisation is based upon the pretence of knowing. Those who know are elevated to the status of gods. It is as though we believe that if we could only discover and name every object and fact in the universe, we could finally be happy.

I have, for a long time now, held the view that if we reverse most things that are considered to be true we begin to approach what really is true. The world in general honours and rewards those who are least deserving of being honoured and rewarded, while at the same time making sure that anyone who really does deserve honour and reward actually receives the opposite.

Because of our reliance and dependency on knowing, we now assume that not knowing is a state of chaos or that it will reduce us to a vegetative state of moral collapse. None of this is true.

Knowing is intrinsically uncreative; its function is to compute, to add, subtract and multiply, to gather and store data and to continually add to the store of data already gathered. In all of these respects it is a wonderful tool.

No matter how much data is gathered and stored, it can never prepare us for the death of others or ourselves, nor even of the death in each moment. Death in each moment refers to all the mini-deaths we experience throughout life. Every loss we experience is a kind of death. Even a small loss is somehow connected in our minds to the final loss, which is death. All roads lead to Rome.

Think of all the people that have entered your life up until this moment in time and who are no longer in your life. These people could be family, lovers, friends, colleagues, or acquaintances. They could be anyone you have had any kind of contact with in your life. And not only people – there may have been pets we have loved or even some object or possession we have valued and lost.

Pain is a message that reminds us that we do not know and that we will die. When we choose to avoid pain and death, we choose to live our lives in fear and deception. Fear of death or of not knowing causes us to seek to know and to control.

We have no control. This is experienced early in our lives and is never forgotten, although we spend the rest of our lives denying this fact and constructing ever more elaborate strategies to prove that we are in control.

There is no solution to death. Death is the solution to life. Death is change and movement. When someone dies they are changed and so are those that are left behind. We do not like these changes. The changes don't need to be liked, they are merely the truth.

Every loss in our lives reminds us of the final loss that is death.

A young child seeing his mother leave the room experiences grief; for him it is as though she no longer exists. At the same time as the child experiences grief he also experiences a loss of power, a diminishment of himself. For the child it is not only that his mother has left the room but that she has left him.

Mankind's universal solution to death is control, or the wish to know. In a universe that is ultimately unknowable, we invent a system that is so convincing that we are able to deny death without a second thought. The first thought is usually more than enough.

The act of thinking is the act of controlling.

During a near death experience (drowning), I inadvertently discovered my ego's inability to deal with death and the fear and pain that go with it. There was a moment when it became clear that the ego could not possibly solve this particular problem. In the moment of that clarity something happened that changed everything, including my certain death. I found that a part of my mind was awakened, that totally accepted the reality of my situation without any fear or desire to change it. In this perfect clarity I could see the means by which I could change it if I wished. It was the most natural thing at this point to want to live, not because I was afraid to die but only because, for the first time in my life, I could see the possibility of living without conflict.

A parable told by the Buddha

A man travelling across a field encountered a tiger. He fled, the tiger after him. Coming to a precipice, he caught hold of the root of a wild vine and swung himself down over the edge. The tiger sniffed at him from above. Trembling, the man looked down to where, far below, another tiger was waiting to eat him.

Two mice, one white and one black, little by little started to gnaw away the vine. The man saw a luscious strawberry near him. Grasping the vine with one hand, he plucked the strawberry with the other. How sweet it tasted.

Pain

When the mind creates the illusion of time, space and movement, it also creates the illusion of pain. As with music, there is only ever one sound possible in any moment, yet by linking a number of notes or sounds together and retaining the memory of each succeeding note, the illusion of music is created. In the same way, pain prior to thought is only sensation; it is the act of linking the memory of each sensation to the next and giving these sensations names and meaning that creates the illusion of pain.

Sensation is neither good nor bad; in fact, without thought, pain is no longer experienced as pain. Prior to thought, sensation is experienced, as something that arises and passes away, that fluctuates in intensity and that is not as terrible as we have believed.

When sensation is fully experienced without the interference of thought, a gate is opened that connects us back through every experience of pain and fear that has occurred in our lives. When sensation is fully experienced all the pain and fear of our lives begins to be processed or completed.

When physical or mental pain is repressed it is left uncompleted. The fact that it is repressed does not mean it is not active; it becomes active in an unconscious way. Over the course of our lives, every experience of pain is repressed and stored and then added to, all the time becoming more powerful.

When pain is repressed so is joy. When pain or sensation is fully experienced or accepted then joy can again enter our lives. Joy is the ability to feel what we feel regardless of what those feelings may be. The ability to feel is the ability to live.

It is necessary to allow pain into our lives. To avoid pain is to avoid freedom and life. It is not necessary to seek pain, it arises naturally and we only need to welcome it when it does arise. To welcome pain is to accept, allow and even to want pain.

A mind that has an aversion to pain is a mind that is averse to truth.

When pain is repressed so is feeling. When feeling is repressed it takes more and more extreme strategies to elicit any feeling at all.

Violence and anger arise of necessity because we are unable to feel. If we are unable to feel naturally, we need to construct feelings in such a way as to convince us that we are alive and able to feel. Alcohol, drugs, sex and violence all become necessary to create the illusion that we are alive.

Our lives reflect the movement between what is and what should be, the movement between now and the future, or past. Within this movement all illusions such as pain, fear and death arise.

There is no truth in the past or future. Truth can only exist in the present. The present is the truth, not our conception of the present, but the present as it is. If we try to describe the nature of the present we turn it into a thing of the past and a thing of the past is a dead thing.

Pain is the conflict that occurs when the ego denies that which is, in favour of that which should be.

Conflict is a major clue that something is wrong, it is a sign that we are beginning to dream and that the dream is being experienced as reality.

Is That So?

Zen master Hakuin was praised by his neighbours as one living a pure life. A beautiful Japanese girl, whose parents owned a food store, lived near him. Suddenly without any warning, her parents discovered she was with child.

This made her parents very angry. She would not confess who the man was but, after much harassment, at last named Hakuin.

In great anger the parents went to the master. 'Is that so?' was all he would say. After the child was born it was brought to Hakuin. By this time he had lost his reputation, which did not trouble him, but he took very good care of the child. He obtained milk from his neighbours and everything else the little one needed.

A year later, the girl-mother could stand it no longer. She told her parents the truth – which was that the real father of the child was a young man who worked in the fish market.

The mother and father of the girl at once went to Hakuin to ask for forgiveness, to apologise at length and to get the child back again.

Hakuin was willing. In yielding the child, all he said was, 'Is that so?'

The Monk and the Teapot

About three days into a meditation retreat I come downstairs from the meditation hall. There will be a tea break after which a monk will give a talk on meditation. Each day someone is assigned to fetch tea from the kitchen; the tea is already prepared. On this day the person assigned to fetch the tea goes to the kitchen and returns soon after, but without the tea. He tells the monk who is to give us the meditation talk that he cannot find the teapots. The monk goes over to the kitchen and returns almost immediately. I am standing around waiting for the tea to arrive. The monk walks past me, he appears to be mumbling. What I hear him say is 'some people can't see what is right in front of their eyes'.

I don't know if this monk meant for me to hear him, or what he meant, I only know that his words had a profound effect upon me.

These words seem to touch a nerve in me; I can't shake them. What is it that is right in front of my eyes that I can't see?

Why Meditate?

Sanity or insanity is the degree to which we believe our own thoughts. Some years ago I experienced something very strange. My thoughts seemed to spontaneously slow down; they seemed to arise in my mind in slow motion. I began to see clearly the nature of my own thinking process. I noticed, first of all, that my thinking almost never stops; as one thought arises, I am already creating the next. It is as though I cannot bear to live without knowing what I will be doing next. There is no particular meaning to most of these thoughts other than to create the illusion that I am in control.

Even though these thoughts have no particular meaning, I find that I am not only giving them meaning but acting on the meaning. Very subtly I create a reality that I am then forced to live. Often, when working with clients I hear them use language that creates the reality they then have to live; a language that begins with a thought. The most common thought or language I hear is, 'I am not good enough', or some variant of this. It seems to me that these thoughts are designed to reinforce, every day of our lives, certain mistaken ideas about who we are. It is important to observe these thoughts or words as they arise and to slowly learn not to invest them with meaning.

As we begin to do this we find that we are not quite so dominated by our thinking.

Slowly we see that thought has no particular meaning; it is a tool that we can use or not use. There is no freedom if the tool uses us. For me, meditation is not a spiritual practice; rather it is a practice that is necessary for mental health.

Meditation can free us of the domination of our own thoughts; it can free us from the domination of the ego. It frees us not by denying or stopping our thinking, but by seeing without judging exactly what we are thinking. Internally and externally we are in constant movement, mostly because we cannot bear to be still. If we are still we begin to experience feelings and sensations we consider unpleasant. A good example of the feelings I am referring to here are those feelings we experience when we are alone in a room with someone and neither you nor they are talking.

The movement of the mind is a smokescreen designed to keep our attention focused away from what is real or true.

Meditation is the act of stopping. If we stop, or even only intend to stop, we begin to experience what a drug addict or alcoholic might experience when they stop taking drugs or alcohol. This is not a pleasant experience, although with meditation it is, and should be, a more gentle experience.

What we see when we meditate is the extent of our neurosis, or disease. Seeing this is not easy; we want to look away; we want to be distracted. When we are able to look into this mirror without looking away we begin to see the truth of who we are; we begin to experience a world that is free of projections of who we are and who we believe others to be.

These projections always result in pain because they are not true.

The result of believing something that is not true ultimately results in pain. What is not true does not 'work'.

When someone believes they are unlovable they believe something that is not true. Others may have convinced them that it is true, but this is not proof. More likely, it is true that whoever it is that convinces you that you are unlovable has been convinced themselves that they are unlovable.

When our neurosis is allowed to continue unchecked, the mind and body are subject to a bombardment of untruth. It is our own beliefs that are untrue. What we call a nervous breakdown is usually a state where the mind has accumulated so many untruths about the world or ourselves that it collapses. The mind can sustain only so many untruths before it breaks down, it stops working in a healthy manner. It seems we can maintain quite a high level of untruth without breaking down. This is not to say we are not in the process of breaking down.

Meditation is more about seeing what is untrue than true. When we see all that is untrue, what is left is the truth. Meditation is the intention to see the truth of who I am, no matter what that truth may be. What we are is less a problem than is the denial of what we are.

Zazen Meditation: a Personal View

In Zazen meditation one sits facing a wall, a plain wall that has no patterns to distract the mind. Facing this wall the sensory world is diminished, there is no longer the stimulus to the eyes and mind that usually distracts us from who we are. There is a reduction of stimulus from the outside; now everything that arises comes from the inside. One is thereby faced with oneself.

From the inside there arise feelings, thoughts and physical sensations. Boredom, sleepiness and pain can also arise. These are all the defences of the mind. Usually when these defences arise we either indulge in them or suppress them. The mind will seek to use all these as distractions that take us away from the moment. In meditation there is the opportunity to work through them. 'Working through' means to process these feelings, thoughts and sensations, by allowing them to complete themselves without any attempt to change them.

In the beginning the mind is full of defences (thoughts running wild, pain in the knees or back, etc.); slowly this begins to subside. As one stays with it our persistence wins out. As we allow that which is to arise with mindfulness, it begins to diminish; it comes because we indulge in it or repress it. Defences arise when we feel threatened; meditation is seen as a threat by the mind. The threat is that we may begin to feel.

The feelings, emotions and pain that arise are not only related to the present, they are also related to the past and to all our experiences in the past.

In the early stages of meditation, there is the observer that sits and watches and evaluates. The observer is the ego and the ego is the originator of our defence systems. When we stop engaging with this system it begins to lose its power and as a result of this, we begin to experience more freedom in our lives.

The ego is the product of fear and as the ego loses its power through meditation, fear also begins to diminish. In essence, the principle of this is that the ego is primarily a defence system against

61

unwanted feelings, so when we begin to allow these feelings the ego becomes redundant; it no longer has a function because what was denied is now allowed.

When we stop labelling what arises there is just that which arises. Pain without label, or without resistance, is free of conflict and simply becomes physical sensation that has no particular meaning.

The process of meditation begins to be mirrored in daily life; things arise in relationships or at work and this process of 'experiencing without judgement' begins, which is to experience truth. As we go deeper into this process of allowing rather than resisting, a new kind of learning appears, not of the intellect but of the body. In this process there is nothing negative; all things begin to teach.

Every area of life is touched. This is not to say that we can control anything; it's saying that life will give us certain experiences, sometimes pleasurable, sometimes painful and many others in between. Instead of fighting or seeking these experiences, we can allow them to occur; as we do this, conflict is diminished and there is a sense of more freedom and lightness in our lives.

Faced by the wall (cinema screen), we begin to project like a cinema projector, all that we are. That is our thoughts, feelings, physical sensations and dreams. The film is seductive, it draws us in and we begin to lose consciousness of the present. At some point, sometimes abruptly, consciousness returns; we are back in the present. How long will it be before we leave again?

Important aspects of this meditation are to really let go and relax; allow yourself to be what you are; completely allow every aspect of yourself, including your thoughts, physical sensations, sounds, pain, sleepiness, restlessness and boredom; also those times when you are more present and more awake.

Adopt a posture that is neither too rigid nor too relaxed, a posture that reflects wakefulness. It is important to be gentle and compassionate with yourself in this practice. In the end it is compassion that is the key – without this we will fail. Compassion requires that we gently accept all that we are. This means all thoughts, feelings, sensations; that which we like about ourselves and that which we don't. It means totally accepting our darkness as well as our light. When we reach this level of acceptance we are free. Conflict signifies that there is something that we do not accept about ourselves.

Keep your eyes open; when we close our eyes we are more likely to dream and not be aware that we are dreaming. When you meditate with your eyes open it is easier to remain connected to the world and to the present and easier to recognise when we begin to dream. The stimulus is reduced but you are still connected and you feel that. Be aware that if your eyes start playing tricks or become unfocused, you are drifting; gently come back.

One of the defences that can arise is sleepiness; it becomes very difficult to keep our eyes open. This is something to be faced, it is a resistance; it is the mind saying, 'Go to sleep. You don't want to do this; you don't want to sit facing this wall. You could be doing something else; you could at least be sleeping.' Work gently with these defences by allowing yourself to close your eyes for short periods, then gently come back to the meditation; it sometimes helps to follow your breathing for a short while.

The void is about the way we reconstruct the world. We reconstruct the world because the world as it is causes us pain. Our reconstruction of the world involves reconstructing ourself. The ego is the architect of this reconstruction. In meditation we start to break through that reconstruction to what could be called the void. Because it is beyond or behind the reconstruction, it is not possible to name this because once it is named it is no longer the void. This void is not empty, but full of life, intelligence and meaning.

There is a Zen saying, that, in the beginning a mountain is a mountain, then it is no longer a mountain, then it is a mountain again.

It is like a circle, it appears that you haven't gone anywhere, but actually you have gone everywhere and the mountain is not the same mountain it was in the beginning; something incredible has happened in the process of going to 'it is not a mountain'.

The essence of the meditation is to be awake. When we are not awake or when we begin to dream or to think, there always comes a moment when we stop and return to the present, although not necessarily because we wish to. It is as though we are attached to a rubber band and as we begin to dream we move away from ourselves; as we move, a tension begins to build up until the force is so great that we are taken back to where we started.

This is the meditation: be aware of that moment when you come back. The more we meditate the more we return to and see the significance of that moment.

Meditation is the act of surfing the present, free of description, judgement, resistance and knowing.

Imagine that from the moment of birth we find ourselves falling through space. We do not know where we are falling from or falling to; we are just falling. In this situation it seems normal that we should project forward and attempt to know the future. We cannot know the future, so we are faced with the fact of falling. If we were to stop projecting either forward or backward, falling would become flying.

Meditation is the act of facing ourselves as we are.

Facing ourselves as we are, we are able to see the ways in which we defend ourselves. These defences take the form of thought, pain, discomfort, boredom, tiredness and even apparently positive spiritual experiences.

All these defences are designed to divert our attention away from the present and away from the pain that resides at the centre of our being.

Uncomfortable feelings and thoughts arise in order to distract us from meditation. It is how we deal with this distraction that is at the heart of meditation. Spiritual experiences can have a more subversive aim – to take control of the whole enterprise.

The most important requirement for meditation is to just sit; to face ourselves as we are, no matter what defences the mind employs. The defences will drop away when the mind finally accepts that they do not work. The clouds will dissolve to reveal a clear sky. This is not some idealised state; it is rather the mind/body in its natural state, free of illusion and free of dependency on the illusions of the mind.

When the mind is free of defences it is also free of conflict. To be free of conflict we must accept conflict. The denial of what is, or truth, is the root of conflict. When we accept the physical nature of our conflict we accept the truth, we become true to ourselves and conflict is no longer necessary.

Escape Velocity

Imagine the earth is the ego, it is immense and powerful; its gravity keeps us firmly on the ground. Beyond the atmosphere of the earth lies space. It is our task to leave the ego/earth behind and enter this new dimension where different rules apply. It is not so easy; we cannot jump into space, even climbing the highest mountain leaves us hundreds of miles away from it.

We can build rockets to take us into space, but this requires a specific amount of energy in relation to the amount of mass that is to be carried. This energy has to be able to move the rocket at a very specific speed; too little and the rocket will fall back to earth. The amount of energy needed to achieve this feat is enormous. The velocity required is also enormous; it is called escape velocity. Imagine we are the rocket that needs to reach escape velocity so as to be free of the influence of the earth/ego.

For me, meditation is the vehicle or rocket that will transport me into space. The energy to be used will be obtained through the process of meditation. When the right amount of the right type of energy is created we will already be on our way. When we reach a certain point on this journey we cannot fall back, we have reached escape velocity.

We now enter a new dimension of being in which the ego does not dominate or determine what we are or what we do. We are free. In space we are weightless, it is silent and still and we have a very new perspective on our place in the universe.

The Long and the Short of it

Recently, during a meditation retreat, I experienced a kind of regression; in regard to my meditation practice I felt like I had gone back a couple of years. I found I was experiencing a restless mind along with waves of drowsiness. In recent years these phenomena had virtually died away.

The retreat was held over a weekend, from Friday evening to Sunday afternoon. All through Friday and Saturday I experienced my mind as restless with continuous bouts of drowsiness. On Saturday evening, after the last meditation of the day, I had a sudden insight. I was answering a question from a group member when it occurred to me that the process of meditation could be likened to long-term and short-term memory. When we sit in meditation we are faced with all the feelings from the recent past that have not been processed. These feelings are at the forefront of our consciousness. These unprocessed feelings are experienced as a restless mind, thoughts racing through our heads and sometimes as physical pain. This feels very uncomfortable; we may feel that we are meditating badly and feel a sense of hopelessness. It is probably this experience that puts many people off meditation. This state is, I believe, predictable – just as when we dream at night we are attempting to process the recent past. The time it takes for this content to be processed is different for each individual. It would be determined by a person's ability to process their feelings, as well as the intensity of the original experience.

An immediate aspect of our state of consciousness can be seen in the way that we experience the wall. The wall may begin to fade and shimmer; sometimes the wall may even disappear. The wall is a precise mirror of our state of consciousness. What we see is what we are. At the time, I was not fully aware of the implications of what I had said.

The next day, Sunday, I began to meditate and found that my mind was very still; I was not at all drowsy or restless and the wall stayed in focus and crystal clear. It was only after the last meditation of the retreat that I began to understand what had been happening.

I am diabetic and about three weeks ago I was sent a letter from the consultant dealing with my diabetes, asking me to see him to discuss the findings of a recent CT scan. During this meeting I was told that a tumour had been discovered in my kidney. I was sent for two more scans to investigate lesions in the liver and pancreas.

After the first of these scans I was told that there was a possible tumour in the adrenal. I was also told that both the kidney and the adrenal would have to be removed in two separate operations. Then I was told that I would be referred to a specialist to further investigate my pancreas. Two days later, I had the second scan; this time I was told that the kidney would still have to be removed but that the other two lesions were not a problem. After this I was sent another letter stating that there was still concern over the pancreas and I would be referred to a specialist.

So this was what was occurring for me directly prior to the retreat; I was on a roller coaster ride, which seemed like life was being given, and then taken away almost every other day. I felt I had been given a death sentence. Although I thought I had been processing this well, I was clearly not processing it as well as I thought. What surprised me was that, given the enormity of what I had been told, I was able to process the events of the last few weeks during the course of the Friday evening and Saturday.

When we sit in meditation we have to sit through this unresolved short-term content and we need to do this with compassion and acceptance; maybe they are the same thing in the end. Faced with a restless, agitated and drowsy mind I was able to accept my state rather than resist it or expect it to be something else; this is the process. When it happens, we are automatically shunted to the next level, which involves the processing of deeper and older feelings. We cannot fully begin this phase of process until the short-term part is complete or up to date.

In the first phase the process tends to be quite turbulent, whereas in the second phase there is a deep sense of stillness. This stillness could not be described as empty. It could be likened to the ocean where on the surface there is a violent storm, yet not far below all is still.

Is it Safe?

Imagine a man moving from one stepping stone to another, across the abyss of death. This man has only one purpose – to get to the next stepping stone. In his imagination he can only see the stones behind and ahead of him. As long as he concentrates on the stones he does not have to look down and he will feel safe.

Knowledge and power are necessary to create the illusion of control.

Knowledge and power are created by thought, the ego and the intellect and are expressed in 'I like', 'I dislike', 'I know', 'I will' and 'I choose'. With each of these the stepping stones are created. There is really no one to step across the stones or even any stones to step across. Even death has become a stepping stone.

Responsibility is the ability to respond rather than to react.

To respond is to move in accord with our senses, our mind and body in unity. This can only be done in the present. To react is to move only in accord with our intellect or ego. To react is to act according to the experiences of the past. To respond is always complete, never partial. To react is always partial and never complete.

The sum of our incomplete actions is manifested as pain in others and ourselves. When we say that someone makes us angry or sad we are denying responsibility for our own feelings. Blaming another for how we feel is a refusal to accept the feelings we have. Another may trigger these feelings but they do not cause them. If we were not already angry no one could 'make' us angry.

When we accept that the feelings we have are ours, we become able to respond. This is not to say that others are not responsible, rather that others are responsible for what they do and feel in exactly the same way we are.

When we deny these feelings and push them on to someone else, we are reacting automatically, the same way that Pavlov's dogs reacted to the sound of a bell by salivating.

Two people reacting to each other (or most of the human race) are in chaos. A person who can respond to another person who reacts is an expression of hope and the possibility of something new.

If I feel angry and then blame someone for causing me to feel this way, a dream is created in which there is no truth. I then have to inhabit this dream and accept whatever consequences arise from it.

If someone is angry with me I have to accept whatever feelings arise in me as being independent of the other person. I accept these feelings or body sensations as being completely my own. At the same time, I need to ask myself honestly if there is any truth in what is being said.

Anger is a feeling of power and as such is addictive. Anger, resentment, rage and even frustration become valid strategies to feel powerful. If we lose power it becomes necessary for the ego to regain it.

Power lost can never be regained; the ego can, however, create a substitute. This false power is never real power; it has no relationship to anything truthful. In the absence of real power it will do.

The creation of anger, resentment and rage is the equivalent of harvesting a drug that will create in us the illusion of power. If this is so, how might we create conditions that would be most fruitful for this endeavour?

It is important to remember that loss of power and replacement of power occurs at an unconscious level. Therefore any strategy used to 'harvest' power will also be unconscious.

We will not harvest this drug in a direct way. At times we will circumnavigate the earth to get somewhere that is right in front of our eyes.

If I need to feel anger as a way to feel powerful, I cannot do this openly; it would be too crazy. I will need to make it appear that my anger is valid; that someone else has caused me to feel angry. In this sense it becomes perfectly valid to choose people in my life who will play out this game with me. This is not so hard, as there are always others who need to feel victimised, this being another form of power.

These mechanisms can only work so long as they remain unconscious. If we can make the unconscious conscious and this without judgement, then the illusion begins to fall apart.

In essence, the mechanism is that, faced with feeling powerless (which is a fact of life), we consciously or unconsciously choose the opposite – to feel powerful. This is not so easy to do; it becomes necessary for the right hand to not know what the left hand is doing.

As a child we expect to feel safe, but sooner or later this expectation is shattered; we find that we are not safe. In fact, we may find that the world we live in is full of hidden dangers. These dangers may be in regard to our physical safety but they are also in regard to our psychological safety.

Our psychological safety is a much more complex problem than our physical safety. The danger is invisible. It is almost as though the mind, not being able to see the danger, is forced to certain conclusions of what the danger is, and also what to do about it. These conclusions are invariably wrong and so too must be the solutions.

A safe world is a dead world. Paradoxically, all wars are the result of mankind's need for safety.

If an idea can give us the feeling of safety we crave, we are prepared to believe anything, no matter how illogical and regardless of how many people may also suffer and die to preserve this idea.

Pain and death deny safety and therefore need to be kept out of sight.

Is it possible to live in the world totally accepting that there is no safety?

We cannot remain as we are, no matter what we think or do. When we attempt to remain as we are, we become fixed or stuck and prone to mental illness. We change even when we try to remain the same.

Life equals change, but change means moving away from what we know. This creates anxiety. We live in a house that is safe, but sooner or later we will need to go out or the house will become unsafe. We are aware that outside the house there are many dangers, yet we take the risk of going out, for to not do so would be more dangerous still.

We are continually faced with the dilemma of wishing to feel safe yet being forced to take certain risks, such as leaving our homes to work, to buy food, crossing the road, driving a car and, the riskiest thing of all, relationships.

Is it safe? No, we can die at any moment. Those we love can also die at any moment. The world can change in the blink of an eye from a seemingly safe and secure place to one of chaos and danger. We will all grow old and experience the deterioration of the body. Husbands, wives, friends or family may leave us. No matter what we do or believe, we cannot avoid any of it. We can lose our jobs, the economy can fail, war can begin. Pick up a newspaper any day of the week and you can read about any of the above happening to someone.

It is not safe. Life is not designed to be safe. It is the element of risk and danger that forces us to grow and life to evolve. The ego is overly concerned with safety and therefore needs to deny the risk factor. The ego replaces risk with the illusion of control and safety. Pretending we are safe and in control is the greatest danger of all. The better we are at creating this illusion, the greater the power of the ego is and the crazier we become.

*In writing this chapter, I was reminded of a scene in the film **Marathon Man**, in which the character played by Laurence Olivier is torturing the character played by Dustin Hoffman. Hoffman is repeatedly asked, 'Is it safe?' Olivier's response to every answer is to inflict more pain on Hoffman and repeat the question 'Is it safe?'*

This scene captures for me the reality in life that no matter what we do or say, it is not safe. We can maintain the illusion of safety for a while, but inevitably, we are faced with pain and death and the illusion is shattered.

When the ego attains a certain amount of power and control it reaches a critical point, where it believes its own imaginings or thoughts to such a degree that it becomes insane. At this point the ego can tell us to harm ourselves or others, commit crimes, start wars, or act in any way we feel like. Dictators, murderers, criminals, terrorists and many who we consider mentally ill, all have this in common; they believe their own thoughts to an excessive degree.

The wiser and more enlightened among us do not believe their own thoughts. Thoughts are seen as clouds passing across a clear sky that have no particular meaning.

Life Choices – Death Choices

Faced with a reality that is unknowable and unsafe we decide to take control. As reality is as it is, we have to pretend that it is something different, that we do have control and we do have the power to make choices. As reality as it is is unacceptable, we make choices that, because they are not related to reality as it is, become death choices, or choices that are not in accord with the truth.

There are many examples of death choices in our lives. Sometimes the choice is literally a death choice – substance abuse, over eating, under eating, violence, crime etc. Two opposing choices made at the same time tend to be death choices; 'I don't like my job, but I am afraid to leave' is a good example. Substitute anything else in place of 'job'. A death choice is a choice made without commitment.

We appear to have made a choice but the result or consequence of our choice does not make us happy. We may continue to make the same choice and not seem to notice that we always end up with the same result. This is strange; in many areas of life we are able to learn from our mistakes. Learning to walk, or even the many different kinds of learning such as reading, writing or maths are examples where we are willing to learn from our mistakes. With drug or alcohol abuse we believe that we don't learn because we are addicted, but is this entirely true? What if we don't learn because we don't want to learn?

Learning, in this instance, would mean experiencing feelings or physical sensations we would rather not. These feelings or physical sensations would not be under our control. It does not matter how negative the things we do may be, as long as they are under our control.

Some years ago, I attended a process-work workshop. At one point we were split up into small groups to practice some of the principles we were learning. In one of these small groups a young woman began banging her head on a table. The facilitator appeared behind her, put his hands on her head and proceeded to bang the young woman's head on the table; the young woman was enraged at this. This is very interesting; why was it OK for her to bang her head but not for someone else to do the same thing? It was OK for her to bang her head because she was in control, but when someone does the same thing to her she is not in control. The belief behind this act is, 'It is OK for me to be harmed, as long as it is me that is doing the harming.'

But why would she choose to harm herself in the first place? I believe it is that she believes she has been harmed in some way, and, unconsciously, comes to the conclusion that if life involves being hurt then it is better if she takes control of doing the hurting. This is a death choice because it creates a no-win situation. To stay in control this woman needs to keep hurting herself.

Ask yourself if you have created something similar in your life. There are so many ways of doing this. Smoking, drinking, drugs, sex, crime and violence are some of the ways we can achieve the same thing. Not fulfilling our potential is also a way of harming ourselves.

Our potential is to live a life in truth and to be what we are designed to be; to not fulfil this will result in pain. This purpose probably does not coincide with the ego's idea of what it is we are designed for. This pain is not only in the future; it is now. Residing in truth we live in a state that is free of conflict. The further away from the truth we are, the more conflict or pain we experience. Pain tells us that we need to attend to this.

The solution is in our hands; it is we who create the conflict and we who can end it. To begin this process we need to look at our choices and see that all that we do is a choice. Perhaps we do not know why we behave in a certain way; this does not mean that we have not made a choice.

We smoke cigarettes not because someone tells us to but because we choose to. We may say, 'I can't stop, I don't have the willpower'; nevertheless there is no one else involved and there is no one else who can change this choice except oneself. I am not saying it is easy; only that if anything is to change it must change with us.

It is a question of responsibility. Most problems arise because of our failure to be responsible. It is so easy to blame our parents, our partners, society, the world, or even God. Blaming others never seems to solve the problem; this is because it is a mistaken view. We are responsible, like it or not.

Even if we deny responsibility we still have to live with the results of our choices. This often results in pain, which again is a clear sign that something is wrong.

It is actually healthier to say, 'I smoke cigarettes because it is my choice. I may not know why, but still it is my choice.' The moment we take responsibility we begin to see more clearly, exactly what our choice is.

Notice when your choice involves two opposing choices. For instance, 'I want to stop smoking but I don't have the willpower.' This involves two choices; the first choice is that I want to stop smoking, the second choice is not 'I can't', it is 'I won't'. Apply this principle to any other dual choice. 'I don't like my job but I don't know what else to do, Translated, this is 'I don't like my job but I will do it anyway, Our lack of responsibility means that we need to fool ourselves into believing that our choice is justifiable. Surely we would not choose something we did not really want?

Converting a dual choice into a single choice is an act of responsibility, even if our choice is to smoke or to work in a job we do not like. A single choice means we are not deceiving ourselves. A single choice also means that the conflict contained within dual choices is released and this helps us see more clearly the exact nature of our choice.

A life choice is a single choice; a choice that we take responsibility for. A life choice arises naturally when we clearly see the death choice. A life choice is always about learning, never about mistakes.

Seeing what we do as a mistake means that we are in conflict and conflict is the enemy of learning. We learn best when we love what we do and are compassionate with ourselves.

Smoke and Mirrors

Look around you; everywhere you look there is madness, people choosing to kill themselves or others and always they have a good reason: 'I smoke because I enjoy it'; 'Who wants to live forever?'; 'It's my only enjoyment'; 'I knew a man who smoked a hundred cigarettes a day and lived to be ninety'. Or, when killing others, 'He/she/they/it deserved it'; 'I was ordered to'; 'They are bad, they are Nazis, infidels, Christians, gooks, inferior, American, English, Russian, Icelanders' – you name it! All the above are clearly crazy, so how do we manage to convince ourselves that we are sane?

It is not so difficult, all it takes is that you believe what you are thinking, saying, or doing. We can always come up with a valid belief no matter what horrors we wish to perpetrate. As we are the one who creates meaning we can create any meaning we like. The moment a meaning is created is the moment when the abstract becomes concrete.

A huge error has occurred in human consciousness; the error is that we believe our own thoughts. We seem not to notice that our thinking is conditioned and therefore suspect. By 'conditioned' I mean that our thinking is clouded by our experiences, by our perception of what we believe occurred. Our thinking is conditioned by the pain or pleasure we receive when young and by everything that is said or done to us.

A computer program is only as good as the data of which it is composed. If the data is faulty then so is the program. In this respect, we are not unlike computers. What is the nature of the information we receive when young? How truthful is it to the way things really are? How truthful are the people giving us this information? How truthful were the people who gave them the information? What strange ideas are accepted as normal within the family? It is not hard to see that our chance of receiving entirely truthful information is very remote.

If we look around us at the world, everywhere we look we see the results of receiving faulty information. How do we reconcile this faulty information with a reality that shows us that faulty information does not work? We invent a system using smoke and mirrors that enables us to believe and do the craziest things imaginable.

We tell ourselves lies, we strategically forget and, most importantly, we believe our own thoughts. The latter enables us to do almost anything we wish, no matter how crazy. We can believe in any number of political systems, from fascism to communism. We can believe in any number of gods or religious systems; we can believe that it is acceptable to lie, steal and kill. We can believe that it is acceptable to slowly destroy ourselves using drink or drugs. We can easily find no contradiction in our religious beliefs and our ability to kill others who do not share those beliefs. Why don't we smell a rat? We don't smell a rat because sometimes we are the rat.

A Map of the Heart

There is a question that arises time and time again in most religious or spiritual teachings; the question is 'Who am I?' It is almost impossible to answer this question unless we actually understand the question. This question cannot be answered in the way we would answer any other question. This question is not being asked of the ego, although the ego will certainly try to answer it.

This question demands a deep inward enquiry, not least as to what the question actually means in the first place. Let us look at what the question is not asking. It is not asking about information as to what your name is, or where you live, or what you like or don't like. This is a very tricky question.

What do you know about yourself that does not involve memory? If we try to answer the question using memory, we are asking the wrong question; it is like trying to catch the wind using a butterfly net. There is also a correlation here of something I touched on earlier – blood washing blood. These are exercises in futility.

Imagine you are looking at an apple and that you have never seen an apple before, there is not even a word for apple in your memory.

How do you find out what this object is? You could look at it very carefully but that will only tell you so much. You could touch it and, again, this gives you a limited amount of information. You could smell it – you get the picture; sooner or later you have to taste it.

Even then we are no nearer to knowing what an apple is, we only have more information about how we may use it. We could look at the apple under a microscope and name all the parts down to the atoms and molecules it is composed of. What we end up with is a rather complex description of the apple and its parts. And still we don't know what an apple is.

The act of eating an apple is the act of knowing an apple, not in terms of a description or words, but as a fact; you could say we experience the apple.

Back to the question 'Who am I?' This question becomes more meaningful to me in terms of what is it that is experienced. This does not mean adding a description such as 'I am angry'; this is not the experience, it is the description. So what is the experience of this thing we usually call anger? Is it possible to experience it without naming it? I have no doubt it is, but it is not easy as we are addicted to naming. We name because naming gives us the illusion that we are in control and that we know.

The title of this chapter refers to a particular aspect of psychotherapy. I think of this aspect in terms of a map, as a multi dimensional representation of the psyche. There are many layers and aspects to this map. It is a map that begins to answer the question, 'Who am I?'

Imagine a table in front of you and on this table there is a map, it is a map of you. For most people this map would be almost blank. There would be areas that you would recognise but these areas would usually contain the aspects of yourself that are memories such as name, address, likes and dislikes and a sequence of memories that tell us about our history. These memories are about all the places and people that have been significant or not in our lives. These memories are not very accurate.

As we begin to see the fine detail in this map we begin to see that there are areas in this map that are blank. We have no knowledge of what is in these areas. In other parts of the map we see that not only is the area unknown but that there is also a prohibition against going into it. We have lived our lives believing that we are free, that we have free will even; now we begin to see that this freedom is illusory. The map has been rigged in such a way that suggests that we are free to do what we wish. Actually what we do is determined by the blueprint that was laid down in childhood.

The blueprint determines everything we do; it contains precise instructions as to what is or is not meaningful. If the blueprint contains the idea that I am unlovable then all my actions will confirm that this is the truth. Think of all the things we can do that can confirm this.

Inherent in this map is the fact of conflict; it is not OK to be who I am. I want to change; I want to be better. This sounds very reasonable to most people – what is wrong with improving oneself? It sounds reasonable but it is not. We will change deeply when we totally accept what we are. When we try to change we inadvertently set up a conflict in the system that will determine that any change we may make will be superficial.

We can move the furniture around but it is still the same room and the same furniture. How many times in the space of a week do you experience conflict? Each time conflict occurs we see a section of the map. The map is not good or bad; it is what it is, it is truth. Conflict suggests that although something may be true, it may also be good or bad; again this sounds very reasonable.

When we add conflict to the truth we not only have to deal with the truth, we now also have to deal with something extra and this is a problem.

For instance, the pain of losing a loved one (which is very natural) can become something far worse; by adding meaning to the experience of grief we can become depressed; we could decide that life is not worth living. We could experience so much pain that we take to drink or drugs.

There is no meaning. Thoughts arise and pass away. Physical sensations arise and pass away. Life arises and passes away.

Everything is in a state of flux, nothing can be held. This is a reality we would rather not know about, it is not possible to know or control this reality. We invent an alternate reality that gives us a strong sense that we are in control, even if that control is negative and destructive. This alternate reality requires that we construct a world of knowing, of naming and of meaning. This in itself is not a problem; it only becomes a problem when we forget that this knowing, naming and meaning are not real; when we forget that we have invented them. When we forget what we have invented we become completely dominated by our own construction and by all the rules inherent in this construction.

At some point in childhood there comes a time when we must make the journey from the child to the adult. This journey is very difficult to do well; ageing itself does not constitute the journey. The journey involves a transition from one state of consciousness to another; it is perhaps the time when the question 'Who am I?' is first asked of us.

When we are young this question is mostly answered with another question, which is 'Who are you?'

We try to find out who we are by checking our view of reality against our parents' or our peers' view of reality. Unfortunately, our parents or our peers have tried to answer these questions in the same way. It is necessary to do this, although at some point we need to move on because the information we have received from others is invariably false.

The information concerning who we are can never come from someone else, it must finally come from within. Others can only give you information about their reality, but not your reality. The information you receive from others is suspect. How do we know that what is being transmitted is true? We can believe; but believing means we do not know.

In meditation we begin to see the extent of our knowing and how this knowing becomes conflict. I begin to experience myself and the world without meaning interfering with the experience; this is not some nihilistic view, it is the truth. When I say without meaning I do not mean this as a negative, as in meaningless. Life is its own meaning. The meaning of life is the fact of life.

A deeper level of this map is related to our internal world of feeling and consciousness. It is only possible to enter this world when the mind is completely still. When the mind moves, it begins to construct a world of knowledge that is based on the past. When this world of knowledge arises the mind finds itself distracted by its own movement and the creations within this movement.

There is a Zen story that refers to this. Two monks are looking at a flag blowing in the wind. One monk says it is the flag moving, the other monk says it is the wind moving the flag. A third monk who overhears them says it is neither; it is the mind that moves.

Drowning was my first experience of what happens when the mind is forced into stillness. I say 'forced' because it was not a choice, it happened because the ego found itself in a prolonged situation in which it had no control. In these conditions the ego collapses, along with all its constructs of fear, pain and meaning. What is left is stillness and clarity and a state of consciousness that is at peace with all that is, even death.

82

This part of the map has no signs or names and it represents more truthfully who we are than any other part of the map. It is a map of the heart.

The map is designed to take you to a specific destination, at which point the map is of no more use.

Exit Stage Left

The world is just a stage and we are all actors. For a time, when we are born on stage, we are not acting. Most of us no longer recall that we were not always actors. Some of us are better actors than others, who now believe in the part they are playing. They train us to also take a part in this play. We resist it but in the end we are drawn into the role that is expected of us. We begin to settle into this role and even begin inventing new roles to play. Some even do this for a living. Early on, we begin to suspect that something is not quite right but decide that what is wrong must be in us.

Pain is the clue that something is wrong. With enough pain we begin to question the play and the actors. In time, we may begin to move away from the stage and take our place in the audience. In the audience it becomes easier to see the nature of the play and to gain some perspective of the roles and the scripts that are being enacted. In time, we become able to predict what will happen next. The play and the acting are very predictable.

At some point it becomes necessary to leave the audience and step back on to the stage. This time it is different; we are no longer seduced by the drama of it all. The actors think we are strange; we no longer know our roles and do not respond in the way that we 'should'. Now our only task is to live in accord with that which is.